PYTHON

PROGRAMMING

A BEGINNER'S GUIDE TO LEARN PYTHON IN 7 DAYS

DAYS

RAMSEY HAMILTON

PYTHON PROGRAMMING
Copyright © 2016 by Ramsey Hamilton

not affiliated with this document.

TABLE OF CONTENTS

INTRODUCTION

I want to thank you and congratulate you for purchasing the book, Python Programming: A Beginner's Guide to Learn Python in 7 Days.

This book contains proven steps and strategies on how to learn Python programming in just a few days. While I don't profess to be able to make you a fully-fledged programmer in that time, my book is aimed at teaching you the basics of Python.

Why Python? Why not C+, Swift, Ruby or Java? There are a lot of very good computer programs out there and each has its pitfalls and its good side. Python is the easiest to learn and once you have a good grounding in it, you can move on to another, more complicated language.

Python is a beautiful computer language. It is simple, and it is intuitive. It comes complete with plenty of libraries and frameworks to help you manage most everything you want to do. And, to back it up, there is a very powerful Python community just waiting to help you out and point you in the right direction.

Python is used by a sorts of people – data scientists use it for much of their number crunching and analytics; security testers use it for testing out security and IT attacks; it is used to develop high-quality web applications and many of the large applications that you use on the internet are also written in Python, including YouTube, DropBox, and Instagram.

Are you interested in learning Python? Then settle in and learn the basics in just 7 days - enough for you to be comfortable in moving on to the next level without any trouble.

Thanks again for purchasing this book, I hope you enjoy it!

Chapter 1:
Setting Up Your Environment

The first thing we must do, before we even start looking at the Python language, is to set up our computer environment. If you use Mac OS X or Ubuntu operating systems then you will find that Python is already preinstalled for you, so for now, we only need to talk about Windows. This first part of the tutorial will work on Windows 7, 8, 8.1 and on Windows 10.

1. Download Python – you will be given the option of Python 2 and Python 3. Which one do you need? In a nutshell, Python 3 is the absolute latest and signifies the direction in which the language I heading, while Python 2 is legacy, has a lot of followers but is not being developed any further, regarding bugs and fixes where needed. Choose the version that suits your needs best

2. By default, you will get the 32-bit version of Python, although you can opt for 64-bit if you choose.

3. Run the Python Installer, choosing **Customize Installation** from the options

4. On the screen that appears, click the boxes beside everything under the heading of **Optional Features** and then click **Next**

5. Under the heading **Advanced Options**, choose where you want Python installed. It doesn't matter where it is, just make sure you remember where.

From here, we have to set up the PATH variable for the system so that we can include the directories that have all the components and packages that we will need later. To do this:

7

- Open your Control Panel
- Locate **Environment** and click on **Edit** under **System Environment Variable**
- Click the button that says **Environment Variables**
- Under **User Variables,** you need to do one of two things – either edit a path that already exists or make a new one. To make a new one, choose PATH as the name of the variable and add the directories listed below to the variable values section. Make sure each one is separated by a semi-colon.
- When you edit an existing PATH, make sure that the values are on separate lines inside the dialog. Click on **New** and input one of these directories on each line:

C:\Python35-32;
C:\Python35-32\Lib\site-packages\;
C:\Python35-32\Scripts\

- Once you have done this, open a command Prompt by clicking on Start>Windows System>Command prompt. When the prompt is open, type in:

Python
This will load up the Python Interpreter ad you should see something along these lines on your screen:

Python 3.5.1 (v3.5.1:37a07cee5969, Dec 6 2015, 01:38:48) [MSC v.1900 32 bit (Intel)] on win 32

Type "help", "copyright", "credits" or license for more information.

```
>>>
```

Because of the way your PATH variable is set up, this interpreter can be run, as can any script, from any of the directories on your computer.

Type in *Exit* and press Enter to come out of the interpreter and back to your command prompt.

Text Editors

The next thing you are going to need is a text editor – you cannot program Python without one. If you use Windows, then you already have one – Notepad. However, there are much better ones that you can use. Do not make the mistake of using Microsoft Word – it is not a text editor and will not save your files in the right format.

For Windows, use Notepad++ and, if you use a Mac, go for TextWrangler.

Windows
- Download Notepad++ from the internet and install it
- Next, to save yourself a lot of work, you'll need to make a change to the Notepad++ preferences file – Open up Settings for Notepad++, choose **Language Menu/Tab Settings**. Next, check the box beside **Expand Tabs** and leave the value as **4**. Click on close

Mac
- Download TextWrangler from the internet and install it
- If you get a message asking you to install some other software or to register, just click on **Cancel**
- Follow the instructions on the screen to set it up, they are very

easy and straightforward.

No matter which one you use, when you are ready to do your first program, save it as **firstprog.py** and remember where you saved it.

CHAPTER 2:
LET'S GET PROGRAMMING

Ok, we have Python installed and we have our text editor, what's next? We get programming! There is nothing worse than reading reams and reams of words about a programming language so I am going to make this is as simple as I can. To do that, I want you to practice what you are learning. As we go through this, you will input the code I give you and see what happens for yourself.

Open IDLE

Open your Start menu and locate Python. Click on it and then run "IDLE. This stands for Integrated Development Environment.

Most of your programming time will be spent in IDLE and you can do a couple of things here – either open a new window for writing a new program or you can play about with single code lines and this is what we are going to do to start with.

In a new window, type in the following code (ignore the >>> as they will already be there)

>>> print "Hello, World!"

Congratulations, you have just created a program that, when executed, will print the words "Hello, Word!" on your screen. When you write these codes, IDLE will automatically compile them so you can see what they will look like – this is useful for testing out code lines, or to see if variables work, etc. More about that later on, though.

Math

The next thing we are going to look at is Math. Type in the following codes – I have given the answers that should be printed on your screen afterward:

>>> *1 + 1*

RESULT

2

>>> *20+80*

RESULT

100

>>> 18294+449566

RESUT

467860

>>> *6-5*

RESULT

1

>>> *2*5*

RESULT

10

>>> *5**2*

RESULT

25

>>> *print "1 + 2 this is an addition"*

RESULT

1 + 2 this is an addition

>>> *print "one kilobyte is 2^10 bytes, or", 2**10, "bytes"*

RESULT

one kilobyte is 2^10 bytes, or 1024 bytes

>>> *21/3*

RESULT

```
7
>>> 23/3
RESULT
7
>>> 23.0/3.0
RESULT
7.6666...

>>> 23%3
RESULT
2
>>> 49%10
RESULT
9
```

So, as you type each code in you should see the result on the screen and it should match with what I have given you here.

Ok, we have Python installed and we have our text editor, what's next? We get programming! There is nothing worse than reading reams and reams of words about a programming language so I am going to make this is as simple as I can. To do that, I want you to practice what you are learning. As we go through this, you will input the code I give you and see what happens for yourself.

Open IDLE
Open your Start menu and locate Python. Click on it and then run "IDLE. This stands for Integrated Development Environment.

Most of your programming time will be spent in IDLE and you can do a couple of things here – either open a new window for writing a new program or you can play about with single code lines and this is what we are going to do to start with.

In a new window, type in the following code (ignore the >>> as they will already be there)

>>> print "Hello, World!"
Congratulations, you have just created a program that, when executed, will print the words "Hello, Word!" on your screen. When you write these codes, IDLE will automatically compile them so you can see what they will look like – this is useful for testing out code lines, or to see if variables work, etc. More about that later on, though.

Math
The next thing we are going to look at is Math. Type in the following codes – I have given the answers that should be printed on your screen afterward:

>>> 1 + 1
RESULT
2
>>> 20+80
RESULT
100
>>> 18294+449566
RESUT
467860
>>> 6-5
RESULT
1
*>>> 2*5*
RESULT

10

```
>>> 5**2
```

RESULT

25

```
>>> print "1 + 2 this is an addition"
```

RESULT

1 + 2 this is an addition

```
>>> print "one kilobyte is 2^10 bytes, or", 2**10, "bytes"
```

RESULT

one kilobyte is 2^10 bytes, or 1024 bytes

```
>>> 21/3
```

RESULT

7

```
>>> 23/3
```

RESULT

7

```
>>> 23.0/3.0
```

RESULT

7.6666...

```
>>> 23%3
```

RESULT

2

```
>>> 49%10
```

RESULT

9

So, as you type each code in you should see the result on the screen and it should match with what I have given you here.

Basic Python Commands

These are the basic commands that you will use in Python programming:

Operators:

Command	Name	Example	Output
+	Addition	5+7	12
-	Subtraction	7-5	2
*	Multiplication	5*7	35
Command	Name	Example	Output
/	Division	12/3	4
%	Remainder	19%3	5
**	Exponent	2**4	16

Remember when you did Math in school and you were taught about the order of operation? That applies to Python programming as well and, if you need a reminder, here it is:

1. Parentheses ()
2. Exponents **
3. Multiplication *
4. Division /
5. Remainder %
6. Addition +
7. Subtraction –

Try these Order of Operation examples:

```
>>> 1 + 2 * 3
RESULT
7
```

The computer will calculate 2*3 first and then it will add the 1 because multiplication comes before addition in the order of operation.

```
>>> (1 + 2) * 3
RESULT
9
```

In this example, 1+2 will be calculated first and then the multiplication. The reason for this is because the code inside the parentheses ha the top priority in the order of operation.

Also, keep in mind that Math is always calculated from the left to the right. The only time it isn't is if it is in parentheses, as in these examples:

```
>>> 4 - 40 - 3
RESULT
-39
```

The first calculation is 4-40, followed by the -3, in the exact order of the code.

```
>>> 4 - (40 - 3)
RESULT
-33
```

In this one, 40-3 comes first because it is inside the parentheses, followed by the subtraction.

Comments

Now, before we move on to doing multi-line programming, there is one last thing you need to know – comments. Type in the following code:

```
>>> #This is a comment. Heed my words!
```

```
RESULT
>>>
```

Notice that there is nothing printed on your screen. This is because a comment, although it is a code, is ignored by Python and is denoted by the addition of a hash at the front of it. Placing the hash will denote everything that comes after it as a comment, but everything before it is normal code. Try this example:

```
>>> print "food is nice" #eat me
RESULT
food is nice
>>># print "food is nice"
RESULT
>>>
```

Nothing, because the code has been placed after the hash, denoting it as a comment.

```
>>> print "food is nice" eat me
```

With this one, you will get an error message because the comment was not placed after a hash.

We use comments to add information to a code for either you or another programmer to read – provided you do it right, only the computer will not be able to read it. You can use comments to explain a piece of code, what it will do or what is wrong with it. One other important use for comments is to place a hash before a piece of code that you don't want to compile yet, but also don't want to delete at this time.

CHAPTER 3:

VARIABLES AND PROGRAMS IN FILES

You know how to do one line coding so let's look at how to send a program to another person so they can use it without having to know how to write it. To do that you'll need your text editor.

It is exceedingly easy to write a program in Python because all they are is a text document and they can be opened in Notepad or TextWrangler so you can have a look at them. So, open your text editor and type in this:

```
#A simple rhyme.
print "The Itsy Bitsy Spider crawled up the waterspout,"
print "Down came the rain and washed the spider out;"
print "Out came the sun and dried up all the rain",
print "the Itsy Bitsy Spider went up the spout again."
```

Type this exactly as it is, with the commas in the eat same places and then save it as **itsy.py**. Make sure that your text editor does not add .txt to the file ending. To stop this, save it as "any file" and, if necessary, turn off "Hide Known File Extensions" through Explorer in Windows if it is easier for you.

Using IDLE
Open up IDLE again and click on **File>Open**. Look for itsy.py and open it. To run the program, click on **Run>Run Module** or you could just press F5. Your program will run in Python and should look like this:

The Itsy Bitsy spider crawled up the waterspout,
Down came the rain and washed the spider out;
Out came the sun and dried up all the rain, The itsy Bitsy spider went up

the spout again.

You can also use IDLE to write your programs, which is what we are going to be doing from now on – we just used Notepad to show that files with the .py extension are merely text files that anyone can look at.

Did you notice that the comment at the beginning wasn't shown? If you typed it exactly as I have, you will not see the words "A simple rhyme". If you didn't put the hash at the front of that, your code will look somewhat messy.

Second, did you spot that lines three and four got joined together? This is because we placed a comma outside of the inverted commas at the end of the text on line three. When you use this in the "print" command, it tells the program not to start another line when showing the text.

Variables

Let's have a look at variables. Think of these as storage containers. Each variable stores a value that you can look at or change later on if you need to. Let's practice using variables. Open up IDLE, click on **File>New Window** and type in the following, EXACTLY as it is:

```
#variables demonstrated
print "This program is a demo of how variables work"
v = 1
print "The value of v is now", v
v = v + 1
print "v is now equal to itself plus one, making it worth", v
v = 51
print "v can store a numerical value, that can be used elsewhere."
print "for example, in this sentence. v is worth", v
print "v times 5 equals", v*5
```

```
print "but v still remains", v
print "to make v five times bigger, you would need to type v = v * 5"
v = v * 5
print "there you are, v now equals", v, "and not", v / 5
Strings
```

As you see, a variable stores the value that you can use later on and you can change them whenever you want to. You don't have to stick to using numbers because a variable can hold text. When it has text in it, a variable becomes a string. Try typing this n:

```
#giving variables some text, and adding more text.
word1 = "Good"
word2 = "Morning"
word3 = "to you too!"
print word1, word2
sentence = word1 + " " + word2 + " " +word3
print sentence
```

The result will be:

Good Morning
Good Morning to you too!

These variables held text. You can also use more than one letter to name a variable – note we used longer names – word1, word2, word3. You can also add strings to make a longer sentence but it will not add spaces in added strings. This is why we added in the "" to denote spaces.

CHAPTER 4:
LOOPS, LOOPS AND MORE LOOPS

Now, what if you needed a program to do the same thing over and over again? How would you do it? Copy and paste the code over and over? That would give you a program that is almost entirely unreadable, slow and, in all honesty, completely pointless. What you could do, is tell the computer that you want to repeat the code between two points until it needs to be stopped. We call this a loop and there are a few of them in Python:

The "While" Loop
Type in this code:

```
a = 0
while a < 10:
    a = a + 1
    print a
```

Now let's talk about how this works by putting that code into plain English for you:

'a' is equal to 0

while 'a' is less than 10, the following should be done:

Make 'a' one larger than what it is already.
print on-screen what 'a' is worth now.

What have we actually done here? When the computer sees a "while" loop, it gets to thinking about what needs to be done. In this code, we have told the computer what "a" is worth. We then told it that while "a" has a value of less than 10, which it does, it should make "a" one bigger – which makes it a "1". We then told it to print the value of "a".

However, because we used the "while" loop, that will continue and the code will print out as ever increasing numbers – 1, 2, 3, 4, etc., all the way up to 10. It stops there because at that point "a" will no longer be smaller than 10 and, as such, the loop is discontinued.

To help you in writing a "while" loop, keep in mind this example:

while {condition that the loop continues}:
   {what to do in the loop}
   {have it indented, four spaces}
{the code here is not looped}
{because it isn't indented}
Type in this example and see what happens:

x = 10
while x != 0:
   print x
   x = x - 1
   print " we've counted x down, and it now equals", x
print "And the loop has now ended."

Boolean Expressions

So, above, where we talked through w to write a "while" loop, you see where we put "condition that the loop continues"? What goes in here is what we call a Boolean expression.

All that means is a question that can be answered with a TRUE or a FALSE response. Let's say that you wanted to put that your age is the same as that of the person sat next to you. Here is what you would type:

My age == the age of the person sat next to me
The response would be TRUE. If your age was lower than the person sat opposite, you would type:

My age < the age of the person sat opposite me

The response would be TRUE. If you were to put that same statement down and the person was actually younger than you are, the response would be FALSE. This is how loops work – if the statement is TRUE, the loop should continue. If it comes up as FALSE, stop looping. Keeping this in mind, have a look at these operators, used in Boolean expressions:

Boolean Operators

Expression	Function
<	less than
<=	less than or equal to
>	greater than
>=	greater than or equal to
!=	not equal to
<>	alternative expression for not equal to
==	equal to

Make sure you do not get = and == mixed up. = makes the left of the operator the same as the right while == is telling whether what is on the left is equal to that on the right and it will return a TRUE or FALSE.

Conditional Statements
Conditionals are pieces of code that will only be run if a set of conditions is met. In many ways this is similar to the "while" loop but instead of many times, a conditional is only run the once. The most

24

common one is the "if" statement and you will find that in any computer language you use. Here is how the "if" statement works:

if {conditions to be met}:
   {do this}
   {and this}
   {and this}
{but this happens regardless}
{because it isn't indented}

Try typing in these examples and see what happens:

Example 1
y = 1
if y == 1:
   print "y still equals 1, I was just checking"

Example 2
print "We are going to show the even numbers up to 20"
n = 1
while n <= 20:
   if n % 2 == 0:
      print n
   n = n + 1
print "there, it's done."

Now, this second example looks a bit trickier, but it isn't really. What we have done is asked the computer to run the "if" statement whenever the "while" loop runs.

'else' and 'elif'

There are lots of ways to use an "if" statement, especially when you are dealing with a situation where the Boolean expression you used comes up FALSE. We are talking about the "else" and "elif" statements.

"else" tells the computer what it should do when the conditions set for the "if" statement are not fulfilled. For example:

a = 1
if a > 5:
  print "This shouldn't happen."
else:
  print "This should happen."

In this example, we have told the computer to print, "This shouldn't happen" only if "a" is greater than 5. If it is less than 5, the computer has been told to print, "This should happen".

"elif" is a shorter way of saying "else if". If the "if" statement is not true, "elif" can be used to tell the computer what to do if the conditions are fulfilled. For example:

z = 4
if z > 70:
  print "Something is wrong"
elif z < 7:
  print "This is normal"

The "if", "else" and "elif" statements all follow this format:

if {conditions}:
  {run this code}
elif {conditions}:

{run this code}
elif {conditions}:
   {run this code}
else:
   {run this code}

There is no limit on "elif" statements that you can use but you can only have a maximum of one "else" statement and that must come after any and all "if" and "elif" statements.

Perhaps the most important thing you must remember is that you must include a colon at the end of any line that has an "elif2, and "if", and "else" or a "while" in it.

Indentation

There is something else that you must remember. Provided the conditions are met, any code that is to be executed has to be indented. This means, if you were to loop five lines using a "while" loop, you must indent by a set number of spaces at the start of the next five lines – this is a requirement in the Python language. Look at this example:

a = 10
while a > 0:
  print a
  if a > 5:
    print "Big number!"
  elif a % 2 != 0:
    print "This is an odd number"
    print "It isn't greater than five"
  else:
    print "this number isn't greater than 5"
    print "and it isn't odd"

```
    print "feeling special?"
    a = a - 1
    print "we just made 'a' one lower than it was!"
    print "and unless a is not greater than 0, we'll repeat the loop again."
print " it seems as if 'a' is now no bigger than 0!"
print "the loop is now over, and so is this program!"
```
Did you notice that there are three indented levels in the code?

Each line in level one starts without spaces – this is the main part of the program and it will always execute.

In the second level, each of the lines begins with four spaces. Where there is a loop or an "if" on level one, everything that is in level two will loop or "if" until there is a new line taking it back to the first level again.

On level three, there are eight spaces at the start of each line. The same thing applies – any loops or "if's" in level two will result in everything on level three looping or "ifing" until a new line starts it back on level two.

That concludes this chapter. I know there is another loop, the "for" loop but we are going to look at that later on.

CHAPTER 5:
FUNCTIONS

In this chapter we need to start looking at purposeful programming, which involves input from a user – that would be you at this stage. And, for user input, we need functions. What are these functions? In effect, they are simply small, self-contained programs that do a particular thing and they can be added into your bigger program.

Once a function has been created, you can then use it in any program to save you a great deal of time. Luckily, Python contains a whole heap of pre-made functions and to use them, you just have to "call" them. When you call a function, you are giving it some input and it will then return a value, similar to the variables, as an output. This is the general format that you use to call a function:

function_name(parameters)

See how easy it is? Function_name identifies the function you are using and the parameters are simply values that you are passing to the function, so it knows what it has to do and how it should do it. For example, let's say we are using a function that multiplies a given number by five, the parameter would tell the function which number to multiply. If you put the number 70 in, the function would output the result of 70*5.

Parameters and Returned Values

OK, so our program can do multiplication but what have we got to show for that? Your program has got to see the result of the multiplication or it has to see if there is an error somewhere – maybe you input a letter instead of a number, for example. How does the function show what it is doing?

Effectively, when a function is run, the computer is not seeing the function name; instead, it will see the result. Remember, this is the same as a variable – the computer only sees the value of the variable, not the name itself. Let's see what we get when we put the number 70 into the brackets – don't bother typing this because the function we are using does not exist, unless we actually create it:

a = multiply (70)

What the computer sees is:

a = 350

Our function ran and returned a number; the answer to the multiplication. Let's try with a real function. You can type this one in and we are going to use the raw_input function. What this does is request a user inputs something which it will then turn into a text string:

 # this line is going to make 'a' equal to whatever you type in
a = raw_input ("Type in something, and it will be repeated on the screen:")
 # this line prints what 'a' is worth
print a

Let's say that, where you were asked to input something, you typed in "Hello". The computer would see this:

a = "hello"
print "hello"

Remember, the variable is nothing more than a value that we stored and, to the computer, "a" looks like the value that has been stored in it. Functions work in a similar way – the man program sees them as the value of the output.

A Calculator

Let's write ourselves a program; a calculator. We are going to get a bit more adventurous than we have so far and we are going to create a program that has a menu in it. The menu will ask what you want to do, giving you the option of adding, dividing, multiplying or subtracting two numbers. There is only one problem with this – the raw_input function will return your input as a text string. We don't want the letter 1, we want the number 1 (and there is a difference in Python).

Thankfully we already have the input function and this will return what you type in but it will return it as a number. If you were to input an integer (a whole number), the output would be an integer. And, if that integer was to be stored in a variable, it would be an integer-type variable, meaning you can carry out Math calculations.

So, we want a menu that will be returned whenever you finish your Math calculation. In other words, it has to loop while you insist that the program still runs. Two big hints there, did you spot them? We want an option in the menu for when you type in a specific number and that will involve the input of a number and the use of an "if" loop.

Let's look at the program in plain English first:

START PROGRAM
print opening message

While we let the program run, we do this:

31

#Print the options you have

print Option 1 - add

print Option 2 - subtract

print Option 3 - multiply

print Option 4 - divide

print Option 5 - quit program

ask for the option it is you want

if it is option 1:

   ask for first number

   ask for second number

   add them together

   print the result onscreen

if it is option 2:

   ask for first number

   ask for second number

   subtract one from the other

   print the result onscreen

if it is option 3:

   ask for first number

   ask for second number

   multiply!

   print the result onscreen

if it is option 4:

   ask for first number

   ask for second number

   divide one by the other

   print the result onscreen

if it is option 5:

   tell the loop to stop looping

Print a goodbye message on the screen
END PROGRAM

Got it? Then let's write the program in a language that Python will be able to read and understand:

```
#calculator program

#this variable tells the loop whether it should loop or not.
# 1 means loop. anything else means don't loop.

loop = 1

#this variable holds the user's choice in the menu:

choice = 0

while loop == 1:
    #print the options you have
    print "Welcome to calculator.py"

    print "your options are:"
    print " "
    print "1) Addition"
    print "2) Subtraction"

    print "3) Multiplication"

    print "4) Division"
    print "5) Quit calculator.py"
    print " "
```

```
choice = input("Choose your option: ")
if choice == 1:
    add1 = input("Add this: ")
    add2 = input("to this: ")
    print add1, "+", add2, "=", add1 + add2
elif choice == 2:
    sub2 = input("Subtract this: ")
    sub1 = input("from this: ")
    print sub1, "-", sub2, "=", sub1 - sub2
elif choice == 3:
    mul1 = input("Multiply this: ")
    mul2 = input("with this: ")
    print mul1, "*", mul2, "=", mul1 * mul2
elif choice == 4:
    div1 = input("Divide this: ")
    div2 = input("by this: ")
    print div1, "/", div2, "=", div1 / div2
elif choice == 5:
    loop = 0

print "Thankyou for using calculator.py!"
```

Now that is an impressive piece of programming. Type it directly into IDLE and save it as calculator.py. Run it and have a play around with it. Try lots of options, enter all sorts of numbers – integers and floating point numbers (decimal point numbers); type in some text and see what happens – a big error message is what will happen and your program will stop running.

Define Your Own Functions

Ok, so we can use all these lovely functions that other people have written but what about if you wanted to write your own? You could certainly save yourself a lot of time by writing your own and you can use them wherever you want. This is where we use an operator called "def". Let's have a look at an example:

```
def function_name(parameter_1,parameter_2):
    {this is the code that is in the function}
    {more code}
    {more code}
    return {the value to return to the main program}
{this code isn't in the function}
{because it hasn't been indented}
#remember to add a colon ":" at the end
#of the line that begins with 'def'
```

So, function_name is, obviously, the name of the function you are using. The code that goes in the function is written underneath that line and it must be indented. Forget about parameter_1 and parameter_2 for now, we'll come back to them later.

Functions are independent of the main program because the computer does not see them, it only sees the value that is returned. Functions are, in effect, small programs that we give parameters to. It will then run itself as an independent program and return a value. The program sees that value but not what has happened to make that value. Let's say that your function went on a long trip, came back and said:

```
return "Hello"
```

The only thing the program would see would be "Hello" in place of the function name ad it wouldn't have a clue that the function had just been on a round the world trip. Because the function is separate, it will not see any of the variables in your program and the program won't see the variables that are inside a function. For example, the following function will print "Hello" on the screen and it will return a value of 1234.

```
# Below is the function
def hello():
    print "hello"
    return 1234
# And here is the function being used
print hello()
```

Look at the very last line of the code – what has it done? If you type this program into IDLE you can see exactly what it has done (don't type in the comments). You should see this on your screen:

```
hello
1234
```

What happened? First, when we ran "def hello()", we created a function called "Hello". Second, when we ran the line, "print hello()", the "hello" function was then executed, meaning the code inside the function was run. That function printed "hello" on the screen and then returned 1234 as a value. Lastly, the program sees "print 1234" and that is what it does.

Passing Parameters to a Function

There is just one last thing to over in this chapter – passing a parameter to a function. Now, think back; how did we define functions? Look at this example of a function defined with parameters:

```
def function_name(parameter_1,parameter_2):
    {this is the code that is in the function}
```

{more code}
{more code}
return {value (e.g. text or number) to return to the main program}

Parameter_1 and parameter_2, inside the parentheses, is where the variable names go, the variables that you intend to put parameters into. Use as many as you want, just make sure you separate each one with a colon.

When the function is run, the first value inside the parentheses will go into the first variable, the second into the second, and so on, for as many parameters as you have included in the function. For example:

def funnyfunction(first_word,second_word,third_word):
   print "The word created is: " + first_word + second_word + third_word
   return first_word + second_word + third_word

So, when you run this function, you would type in something along the lines of:

funnyfunction("meat", "eater", woman")

The first value goes into variable one, the second into variable two, and so on. This is how we pass a value, or a parameter, to a function from a program – by putting them after the function name, in the parentheses.

Finally

Let's go back to our neat calculator program. Did it look a little on the messy side to you? It did to me so we are going to write it again but using functions this time. We will use the "def" operator to define all of the functions we will need. Then, the main program will look better, with all that messy looking code changed over for neat, tidy functions. This will make it easier for the future:

```
# calculator program

# NO CODE IS RUN HERE, IT IS TELLING US WHAT WE WILL DO
LATER
# Here we will define our functions
# this prints the main menu and prompts for a choice
def menu():
    #print what options you have
    print "Welcome to calculator.py"
    print "your options are:"
    print " "
    print "1) Addition"
    print "2) Subtraction"
    print "3) Multiplication"
    print "4) Division"
    print "5) Quit calculator.py"
    print " "
    return input ("Choose your option: ")


# this adds two numbers given
def add(a,b):
    print a, "+", b, "=", a + b


# this subtracts two numbers given
def sub(a,b):
    print b, "-", a, "=", b - a


# this multiplies two numbers given
```

38

```
def mul(a,b):
   print a, "*", b, "=", a * b


# this divides two numbers given
def div(a,b):
   print a, "/", b, "=", a / b


# NOW THE PROGRAM REALLY STARTS, AS CODE IS RUN
loop = 1
choice = 0
while loop == 1:
   choice = menu()
   if choice == 1:
      add(input("Add this: "),input("to this: "))
   elif choice == 2:
      sub(input("Subtract this: "),input("from this: "))
   elif choice == 3:
      mul(input("Multiply this: "),input("by this: "))
   elif choice == 4:
      div(input("Divide this: "),input("by this: "))
   elif choice == 5:
      loop = 0


print "Thankyou for using calculator.py!"


# NOW THE PROGRAM REALLY FINISHES
```

The first program you write had 34 lines of code. This one had 35 so how can it possibly be neater? It is longer but look at it, doesn't it look so much simpler? All of your functions got defined at the start and, as you know, they are not part of the program, just little programs that you are going to use later on.

Now look at the man program. Between "loop = 1" and "print Thankyou…" there are just 15 code lines. That means, if you wanted to have a go at writing the program again, in a different way, you would only have to write 15 lines instead of the original 34 that you had before we learned functions.

CHAPTER 6:
DICTIONARIES, LISTS, AND TUPLES

Have you got a bit of brain ache after the last, mammoth chapter? Don't worry because this one isn't so bad. We are going to look at variables again bit this time in more detail.

Variables can store a piece of information, we now this. They can spit that information out at any time and we can change that piece of information whenever we want to. Variables are neat things, really good at what they are meant to do -storing information that can be changed.

What if you wanted to store a list of information; something that doesn't change. Say, the months in the year, they don't change. Or you might want to store a list of information that can change, like your cats' names – some will die, you could get a new one, etc., or a list of friends and phone numbers. This isn't quite so easy and will require a bit of referencing on your behalf. You will have a list of the names and a phone number for each one in the case of your contacts. How are you going to do this?

Dictionaries, Lists, and Tuples
That's how you are going to do this.

Three problems; three solutions.
- Lists - exactly what they say they are. Lists of values. Each one has a number, in ascending order and beginning from zero. Value can be removed and new ones added in when needed.
- Tuples - similar to lists but the values cannot be changed. Make sure you give them the right value first time around because you

are stuck with it. Each value is numbered, beginning at zero.

- **Dictionaries** – quite similar to what you would expect them to be – a dictionary. This includes an index of all the words and a definition of each one. In the Python language, words are called "keys" and the definitions are called "values". Values are not numbered in dictionaries ad they are not in any particular order. Keys can be added, removed or changed in a dictionary.

Tuples

These are actually quite easy. You provide your tuple with a name and then you list all of the values that will be in it. Let's use our previous example, the months of the year:

*months = ('January', 'February', 'March', 'April', 'May', 'June', \
'July', 'August', 'September', 'October', 'November',' December')*

Note the "\ at the end of the first line? This carries the code over to line two and a nice way of making the code, especially long lines, a bit more readable.

Technically, the parentheses do not need to be there but it helps Python to understand things a little better. And, you can put spaces in after each comma if you want to – it really doesn't make any difference.

Python will take this code and it will order everything in an index, a nice neat numbered index, beginning at zero, and in the order that you put them in. It would look something like this:

Tuple indices
Index   Value

0	*January*
1	*Feb*
2	*Mar*
Tuple indices	
3	*Apr*
4	*May*
5	*Jun*
6	*Jul*
7	*Aug*
8	*Sep*
9	*Oct*
10	*Nov*
11	*Dec*

That is really all there is to a tuple.

Lists

These are similar to tuples but a list can be modified (in computer language, the contents are mutable) and their values can be changed. On most occasions you will use lists, rather than tuples, for the very reason that you can change a thing if you want to.

Lists are defined in much the same way as a tuple. Let's use your cats' name as an example. You have five of them – Smokey, Josie, Jemima, Suzy, and Tom. To list them, you would do this:

cats = ['Smokey', 'Josie', 'Jemima', 'Suzy', 'Tom']

The code is identical to a tuple with one exception – the values are placed inside square brackets, not inside parentheses. Again, it's up to you if you add spaces in after the commas or not, it really doesn't make any difference.

Values are recalled from a list in the same way as a tuple. Let's say you wanted to pull out the name of your third cat, you would do it like this:
print cats[2]
Remember, numbering starts at zero so cat number three would be classed as two. You can also recall a whole range, for example, using *cats[0:3]* would recall the first 4 cats on your list.

Where a list really shines is in the fact that they can be modified. You can add a value to your list by using the "append90" function so, let's assume that you acquired a new cat, called Sukey. To add Sukey to your list, you would do this:

cats.append('Sukey')

Hold on. Something doesn't look right there, does it. The function isn't where you would expect it to be, after the (.) after the name of the list. We will look at this in a later chapter but, for now, this is the right format for adding a value to your list:

#add a new value to the end of a list:
list_name.append(**value-to-add**)

#e.g. to add the number 5038 to the list 'numbers':
numbers.append(5038)

Does that make it easier to understand?

Now, we have a bit of a sad situation on our hands here. Tom died, he was an old cat. Sad but you now need to remove him from your list. That is easy to do:

#Remove your 5th cat, Tom. How sad
del cats[1]

That removes Tom from your list and, on that sad news, let's move on to the next thing.

Dictionaries

For most people, there is a bit more to life than listing the names of their cats. Most of us have family and friends that we want to call at times and for that, we need a telephone book. The list we looked at can't really be used in this way because we need to now a phone number connected to a name, not the other way around. When we did the cats and the months, the computer was given a number and, in return, it would give us a name. For this, we want to give our computer a name and have it give us the number. This is where dictionaries come in.

So, how do we go about making a dictionary? Remember what I said earlier – dictionaries have keys, instead of names, and each key has a value. In a phone book, you have names and you have a phone number for each name.

When you first create your dictionary, it will seem similar to how you create a list or a tuple. Tuples have (parentheses), lists have [square brackets] and dictionaries have {curly braces}. Look at the example below, of a dictionary containing four phone numbers:

#Make the phone book:
*phonebook = {'Andrew Peters:8806336, *
*'Emily Lemon:6784346, 'Peter Parsons:7658344, *
'Lewis Locke:1122345}

Your main program will print the number for Lewis Locke on the screen. Notice that, rather than identifying a value using a number, instead, we identify the value with another value, a name of a person in this case.

So, you have created your phone book now you need to add a new number. To do that, we use a very simple piece of code:

#Add the person named Pinocchio' to the phonebook:

phonebook[Pinocchio'] = 1234567

 # You didn't think I would give you
 # my real name and number now, did you?

What this line is saying is, we have a new person called Pinocchio in the phone book and he has a phone number of 1234567. Pinocchio is the key; the phone number is the value.

You can also delete entries from a phone book in the same way as you do with a lit. Let's say that Andrew Peters is your next door neighbor and he moves away. You won't need his number again so, to remove it, you would do this:

del phonebook['Andrew Peters]

Again, another easy thing to do. The operator "del" will delete functions or entries in lists and dictionaries. Remember this for later on – a dictionary entry is a variable that has a text or number string as its name.

Now, remember we talked about the "append" function earlier? We can use a number of these with a dictionary. Take a look at this program, incorporating some of the functions. I have also included comments to help you along but, if you opt to type this into IDLE yourself, don't include the comments.

```
#A couple of examples of a dictionary

#First we must define the dictionary
#it will not have anything in it this time
ages = {}
#Add four  names to the dictionary
ages['Sue'] = 23
ages['Peter'] = 19
ages['Andrew'] = 78
ages['Karren'] = 45


#Use the function has_key() -
#This function takes this form:
#function_name.has_key(key-name)
#It returns TRUE
#if the dictionary has key-name in it
#but returns FALSE if it doesn't.
#Remember - this is how 'if' statements work -
#they run if something is true
#and they don't when something is false.
if ages.has_key('Sue'):
   print "Sue is in the dictionary. She is", \
ages['Sue'], "years old"

else:
   print "Sue is not in the dictionary"


#Use the function keys() -
```

```
#This function returns a list
#of all the names of the keys.
#E.g.
print "The following people are in the dictionary:"
print ages.keys()

#You could use this function to
#put all the key names in a list:
keys = ages.keys()
#You can also get a list
#of all the values in a dictionary.
#You use the values() function:
print "People are aged the following:", \
ages.values()

#Put it in a list:
values = ages.values()

#You can sort lists, with the sort() function
#It will sort all values in a list
#alphabetically, numerically, etc...
#You can't sort dictionaries -
#they are in no particular order
print keys
keys.sort()
print keys

print values
values.sort()
print values
```

```
#You can find the number of entries
#with the len() function:
print "The dictionary has", \
len(ages), "entries in it"
```

There are loads of functions you can use with dictionaries and lists, this is just a small snapshot of them. We are going to end this chapter here, let your brain have a rest before the next one

CHAPTER 7:
THE "FOR" LOOP

Remember, I said I would come back to this one in chapter 4, so here it is. The "for "loop can be used for every single value in a list. It is set out in a somewhat confusing way but it is actually very basic. Look at this example:

```
# Example 'for' loop
# First, you have to create a list to loop through:
newList = [45, 'eat me', 90210, "The day has come, the walrus said, \
to speak of many things", -67]

# create the loop:
# Goes through newList, and sequentially puts each bit of information
# into the variable value, and runs the loop
for value in newList:
print value
```

Did you notice that, when the loop is executed, it goes through every value that is in the list after "in"? Then, it puts each one into value and then it executes through at loop. Each time, the value is worth something else. Let's look at another example so we can understand better:

```
# cheerleading program
word = raw_input ("Who do you go for? ")

for letter in word:
    call = "Gimme a " + letter + "!"
```

```
    print call
    print letter + "!"
print "What does that spell?"
print word + "!"
```

You should have learned two things here:
- Strings are nothing more than lists with a load of characters
- The program went through every letter, or value, in a word and them printed them on the screen

Really, that is all there is to the "for" loop.

Making a Menu Function

Ok, now you know what they are for, let's look at writing an actual program. We now know all about variables, loops, lists and functions and that really does take care of an awful lot of programming. So, a task:

```
# THE MENU FUNCTION
# The program will ask for a string with all the menu options in it,
# and a text string that asks a question.
# so make sure every menu entry is unique.

def menu(list, question):
  for entry in list:
    print 1 + list.index(entry),
    print ") " + entry

  return input(question) - 1

# def menu(list, question): is telling the function to
# ask for two bits of information:
```

```
# A list of all the menu entries,
# and the question that it will ask when all the options have been printed

# for entry in list: is saying;
#'for every entry that is in the list, do the following:'

# print list.index(entry) + 1 uses the .index() function to find
# where in the list the entry is in. the print function then prints it
# it adds 1 to make the numbers more intelligible.

# print ") " + entry prints a bracket, and then the entry name

# after the for loop is finished, input(question) - 1 asks the question,
# and returns the value to the main program (minus 1, to turn it back to
# the number the computer will understand).
```

That wasn't too tough, was it? Taking out the comments, if you typed this into IDLE, you will have noted that there were actually only 5 lines of code! My comments take up more than three times that. It is always a good idea to make extensive comments on your programs. Not only will you find it easy to understand what you have done but so will anyone else who reads it.

A First Game

So, what will we do for our example program? How about a game? A very simple one; a text adventure. It will be in just one room in the house and it will be very simple. The room will have a door and five things in it. In one of these will be the key to the door and you must find that key to open the door. Let's do it in plain English first and then the proper coding for Python:

#Plain-English version of our 'game'

First, we tell the computer about our menu function

Then we print a welcoming message, with a description of the room.
We will give the player six things to look at: plant, painting,
vase, lampshade, shoe, and the door

We tell the computer that the door is locked
And we tell the computer where the key is

Then we present a menu, telling you what things you can 'operate':
  It will give you the six options
  It will ask the question "what will you look at?"

if the user wanted to look at:
  pot plant:
    If the key is here, give the player the key
    otherwise, tell them it isn't here
  painting:
    same as above
  etc.
  door:
    If the player has the key, let them open the door
    Otherwise, tell them to look harder

Give the player a well-done message, for completing the game.

From this, we can now write the program in Python code -when you type it in, ignore the comments:

```python
#TEXT ADVENTURE GAME

#the menu function:
def menu(list, question):
    for entry in list:
        print 1 + list.index(entry),
        print ") " + entry

    return input(question) - 1


#Give the computer some basic information about the room:
items = ["pot plant","painting","vase","lampshade","shoe","door"]

#The key is in the vase (or entry number 2 in the list above):
keylocation = 2

#You haven't found the key:
keyfound = 0

loop = 1

#Give some introductory text:
print "Last night you went to sleep in the comfort of your own home."

print "Now, you find yourself locked in a room. You don't know how"
print "you got there, or what time it is. In the room you can see"
print len(items), "things:"
for x in items:
    print x
print ""
print "The door is locked. Could there be a key somewhere?"
```

```
#Get your menu working, and the program running until you find the
key:
while loop == 1:
    choice = menu(items,"What do you want to inspect? ")
    if choice == 0:
        if choice == keylocation:
            print "You found a small key in the pot plant."
            print ""
            keyfound = 1
        else:
            print "You found nothing in the pot plant."
            print ""
    elif choice == 1:
        if choice == keylocation:
            print "You found a small key behind the painting."
            print ""

            keyfound = 1
        else:
            print "You found nothing behind the painting."
            print ""
    elif choice == 2:
        if choice == keylocation:
            print "You found a small key in the vase."
            print ""
            keyfound = 1
        else:
            print "You found nothing in the vase."

            print ""
    elif choice == 3:
```

```
        if choice == keylocation:
            print "You found a small key in the lampshade."
            print ""
            keyfound = 1
        else:
            print "You found nothing in the lampshade."
            print ""

    elif choice == 4:
        if choice == keylocation:
            print "You found a small key in the shoe."
            print ""
            keyfound = 1
        else:
            print "You found nothing in the shoe."
            print ""
    elif choice == 5:
        if keyfound == 1:
            loop = 0
            print "You put in the key, turn it, and hear a click"

            print ""
        else:
            print "The door is locked, you need to find a key."
            print ""

# Remember that a backslash continues
# the code on the next line

print "Light floods into the room as \
you open the door to your freedom."
```

That was quite a simple and fun game. Very important – do not let the amount of code get the better of you. Look through it carefully and you will see that 53 of those lines are nothing more than "if" statement, the easiest thing in the world to understand. The most important thing is to get the hang of the indentation business. Once you do, you will understand the code a lot better.

Before we move on, let's have a look at how to make this game better. First, ask yourself if the program works properly The answer should be yes, in which case, ask yourself if it works well. No, it doesn't. While the menu() function is superb, because it takes away a lot of typing, the "while" loop is messier than it should be. There are four indent levels and that is a lot for such a simple program. No, we can do better than this.

When we get around to classes, in the next chapter, things will be so much more straightforward. For now, though, let's create ourselves a function that will tidy up. We are going to pass two things to this function – the key location and the menu choice. In return, the function will return just one thing – if the key has been located or not. Look at this example:

```
def inspect(choice,location):
    if choice == location:
        print ""
        print "You found a key!"
        print ""
        return 1
    else:
        print ""
```

```
print "Nothing of interest here."
print ""
return 0
```

Now we can make the main computer program somewhat simpler. Let's start at the "while" loop and have a bit of a change around:

```
while loop == 1:
    keyfound = inspect(menu(items,"What do you want to inspect?"), keylocation)
    if keyfound == 1:
        print "You put the key in the lock of the door, and turn it. It opens!"
        loop = 0

print "Light floods into the room, \
as you open the door to your freedom."
```

See how much shorter the program is? Down from 83 line to a nice, neat 50. Obviously, we have lost some of the versatility that we built in because, now, everything in the room does the same thing. Instead for having to do it, the door automatically opens when you locate the key and the game loses a bit of interest. Shortening it in this way also makes it harder to change things.

Have a go at writing your own game and see how you get on. Don't forget, writing it in IDLE will allow you to test out each line of code as you write it so in theory, you shouldn't be able to go wrong. Even if you do this is the kind of hands on, practical experience that will teach you how to code in Python.

CHAPTER 8:
CLASSES

If there is one thing that you should learn about programming, it is that on the whole, a programmer likes to be as lazy as possible. After all, if we've already done something, why do we want to do it again? This is where functions come in. Your code has already done something quite special so now you want it to do it again and why not. So, you place that piece of special code into a function and then re-use it as much as you possibly can. Functions can be referred to anywhere in Python code and the computer is always going to know exactly what you are talking about.

Functions do have limits, though. For a start, they cannot be used as a way of storing information, like the lovely little variable. Whenever you run a function, it has to start over again. However, there are some functions and variables that are closely related to one another and they have to interact on many occasions. For example, let's say that you own a nice golf club. You have the information about it, like the length of the shaft on it, the material used to make the grip, and the material used in the head – that information is stored in a variable. However, that golf club also has a number of functions that are associated with it. Swinging the club, hitting the golf ball, even breaking the club because you missed such an easy shot. For those functions to work properly you have to know the information stored in the variable.

With a normal function, that is easily worked out. A parameter has an effect on a function but, what if that function had to affect your variable in some way? What would happen if, whenever you used that club, the shaft weakened, the head got scratched or the grip wore away? Functions can't do this because a function can only have one output.

What we need is a way of grouping together the variables and functions that are related to one another so that they can easily interact with each other.

What if you had several golf clubs? Each one would need all that information written about it separately. So what we really need here is a class; a class that we can use to store information about our clubs, and the functions. That way, we could write some code for each club and then, each time something changes, we just tack on a bit of code, instead of having to write the code over and over again.

It is these problems that can be solved by object oriented programming. This is what puts variables and functions together so that they can see each other and they can easily work together; they can be replicated; they can be modified if needed. This is where the class comes into play.

How to Create a Class

So, what is this class? Think of it as something along the lines of a blueprint. A class isn't actually anything itself, it just describes how you make a thing. From that one blueprint, you can make a whole heap of things and we call this an instance. So how do we make a class? Simple. We use the "class" operator. Look at how to define a class:

 # Defining a class
class class_name:
   [statement 1]
   [statement 2]
   [statement 3]
   [etc]

Does that make a bit more sense? No? Ok, try this example, the creation of a shape definition:

```
#An example of a class
class Shape:
  def __init__(self,x,y):
    self.x = x
    self.y = y
  description = "This shape has not been described yet"
  author = "Nobody has claimed to make this shape yet"
  def area(self):
    return self.x * self.y
  def perimeter(self):
    return 2 * self.x + 2 * self.y
  def describe(self,text):
    self.description = text
  def authorName(self,text):
    self.author = text
  def scaleSize(self,scale):
    self.x = self.x * scale
  self.y = self.y * scale
```

What you have done here is create the description of a shape or a variable and you have defined what you can do with that shape (the function). This is vital – what you have NOT done, is created a real shape, only a description of that shape - look at the code; we have defined a size for the shape – the width height, perimeter, and area. When you define classes, you are not running any code, only making variables and functions.

In this code, the function named __init__ will be run when an instance of a shape is created, or when the real shape is created and not a blueprint. You will gain more understanding of this later on so don't worry if you can't grasp it now.

"self" is the way that we refer to a thing in a class and is the very first parameter in any function that has been created in a class. If you create a variable or a function on the first indent level (code that is one tab into the right of the class Shape), it will automatically be placed into "self". If you want to access any of the variables or functions that are anywhere else in the class, you must make sure that the name of each one is preceded by "self" and a period, or full stop. For example, *self.variable_name*

How to Use a Class
Ok so we know how to make a class but how on earth do we use it? Look at this example first, of an instance created of a class:
rectangle = Shape(100,45)
What have we done? This is going to take some explaining so bear with me.

First, this is where the __init__function really comes out to play We have created an instance of a class by providing it with a name (Shape in this case) and then giving values, in brackets, that are to be passed to the __init__ function. This function will then run, making use of the parameters you have given it inside the brackets. It will produce an instance of the class and, in the case of this example, the instance is assigned to the name, "rectangle".

Ok now, this "rectangle" class. Think of it as a collection of self contained functions and variables. So, in the way that we used "self" to get access to variables and functions in the class instance from within itself, we can use the name assigned (rectangle) to gain access to those variables and functions of the class instance from outside of itself. So to follow on from our last piece of code, we would now do this:

```
#find the area of your rectangle:
print rectangle. Area()

#find the perimeter of your rectangle:
print rectangle.perimeter()

#describe the rectangle
rectangle.describe("A wide rectangle, more than twice\
 as wide as it is tall")

#make the rectangle 50% smaller
rectangle.scaleSize(0.5)

#re-print the new area of the rectangle
print rectangle.area()
```

Did you notice that, where we used "self" from within a class instance, we use the assigned class name when it is outside? The reason we do this is so that we can see the variables inside the class and change them if we want to, as well as being able to access the variables.

We are not stuck at using just one instance of a class, though, we can have as many as we want. For example, we could do this:

```
longrectangle = Shape(120,10)
fatrectangle = Shape(130,120)
```

both of these have their own set of variables and functions inside of them and are completely independent of one another. There really is no limit to the number of class instances that you can create.

The Lingo

OOP, or Object Oriented Programming, has its own lingo and its time we looked at it and learned it:

- When you are first describing a class you **define** it, like you do with a function
- When you can group together similar variables and functions, this is known as **encapsulation**
- When you describe code where a class has been defined, you use the word **class**. However, we also use **class** to describe an instance of the class so be clear which form you are talking about
- Variables that are inside a class are called **attributes**
- Functions inside a class are called **methods**
- Classes come under the same category as variables, dictionaries, lists, etc. in that they are all **objects**
- Classes are known as **data structures** because they hold data and they hold the methods needed to process the data

Inheritance

Just going to back to the start for a minute, we know that a class can group similar functions and variables together (knowns as methods and attributes) so that the data is together with the code that is needed to process it. We know that we can create many instances of one class so that we don't have to keep on repeating ourselves or writing new code for new objects. What about when you want to add things in? This is when the rules f inheritance come into play.

To be fair to Python, it makes inheritance dead easy. The way we do it is, we define a class, based on a parent class, and that new class will then bring in everything that was in the parent. We can add to it as well so, if there are new methods or attributes that share the same name as those in the parent class, they are used in place of the parent. Just cast your mind back a bit to the Shape class:

```
class Shape:
   def __init__(self,x,y):
      self.x = x
      self.y = y
   description = "This shape has not been described yet"
   author = "Nobody has claimed that they made this shape yet"
   def area(self):
      return self.x * self.y
   def perimeter(self):
      return 2 * self.x + 2 * self.y
   def describe(self,text):
      self.description = text
   def authorName(self,text):
      self.author = text
   def scaleSize(self,scale):
      self.x = self.x * scale
   self.y = self.y * scale
```

If we were to define a new class, perhaps a square and we wanted to base it on the previous class, this is what we would do:

```
class Square(Shape):
   def __init__(self,x):
      self.x = x
         self.y = x
```

Really and truthfully, it is like you would define a class normally, but this time we are adding in the parent class that we inherited from. As you can see, this is a really quick way to define a class because everything we need came from the Shape class and we only changed what was necessary. In this case, __init__ was redefined, making the values for x and y identical.

So, taking what you have learned here, let's define another class and this time, we are going to inherit from Square. We will have two squares, one to the left of the other:

```
# The shape will look like this:
# _____
#|   |   |
#|   |   |
#|____|____|
class DoubleSquare(Square):
    def __init__(self,y):
        self.x = 2 * y
        self.y = y
    def perimeter(self):
        return 2 * self.x + 3 * self.y
```

This time, we had to redefine another function, the perimeter, as there is a line that goes down the center of your shape. Now try to create an instance of the new class. A hint for you – the IDLE command line will start where the previous code ended so all you have to do is type in the new lines of code at the end of this last program.

Dictionaries of Class and Pointers

Remember when we said that one variable is equal to another, for example, *variable2=vaiable1* – the variable on the left of the = is the same value as the one on the right. In the case of a class instance, things are a little different. The name that is on the left will become the class instance that is on the right. For example, *iinstance2=instance1* – in this case, instance2 points to instance1. Remember that there are two names that are given to a class instance and you can use either one of them to get into the instance.

Lastly, we look at dictionaries of class. Keeping in mind what we said about pointers just now, we can now assign a class instance to an entry that is in a dictionary or a list. This let you have just about any amount of class instances in existence when the class runs. Look at this example:

 # Again, we assume the definitions on Shape,
 # Square and DoubleSquare have now been run.
 # First, we create a dictionary:
dictionary = {}
 # Then, we create some instances of classes in that dictionary:
dictionary["DoubleSquare 1"] = DoubleSquare(5)
dictionary["long rectangle"] = Shape(600,45)

#You can now use them like you would a normal class:
print dictionary["long rectangle"].area()

dictionary["DoubleSquare 1"].authorName("The Gingerbread Man")
print dictionary["DoubleSquare 1"].author

All we did was replaced our original name that was on the left with a snazzy new dictionary entry/

Chapter 9:
Modules

The last chapter was a bit of a killer so, this time, we will ease up a bit. Remember, if you will, that a class is a nice combination of similar variables and functions that interact with one another, all packed together in a nice neat place. We call this **encapsulation** but, no matter what it is called, it is a nice feature that keeps everything together, allowing you to use the code in lots of instances in lots of places. Now, I know what the next question is – how do we get those classes to lots of places in lots of programs? The short answer is, we use a module that we can then import into another program.

What is a Module?

A module is a file in Python that usually contains definitions of functions, variables, and classes. You might see one look a bit like this:

EXAMPLE OF A PYTHON MODULE
 # Define a few variables:
numberone = 1
ageofqueen = 78

 # define a few functions
def printhello():
  print "hello"

def timesfour(input):
  print input * 4

 # define a class

```
class Piano:
    def __init__(self):
        self.type = raw_input("What type of piano is this? ")
        self.height = raw_input("What height (in feet) is it? ")
        self.price = raw_input("How much did it cost you? ")
        self.age = raw_input("How old is it (in years)? ")

    def printdetails(self):
        print "This piano is a/an " + self.height + " foot",
        print self.type, "piano, " + self.age, "years old and costing\
" + self.price + " dollars."
```

They don't look too much different from a standard program in Python. But what do we do with them? We can import a bit of or an entire module into another program. Write that code above in IDLE and save it as moduletest.py. Now we are going to import it into another program in its entirety. To import this into the main program you were writing, you would do this:

```
### mainprogam.py
### IMPORTS ANOTHER MODULE
import moduletest
```

This is now assuming that the module is either a default one that came included with Python or it is already in the directory that your main program is saved in. You do not include the .py extension – this is always ignored. Normally, you would put together all of the import statements at the start of the file but you can actually put them anywhere you want. If you want to use the contents of your module in your main program this is what you would do:

USING AN IMPORTED MODULE
Use the form modulename.itemname
Examples:
print moduletest.ageofqueen
cfcpiano = moduletest.Piano()
cfcpiano.printdetails()

As you can see, the imported modules act a bit like those classes we learned about in the last chapter. Anything that is inside of one must be preceded by the name of the module if it is to work.

What about if you wanted to get rid of the module name part that has to go in front, though? There is a way to do it. First, you can import only what you want from inside the module, rather than the whole thing. To do this we need to use an operator called "from" and the format you use it in is, *from modulename import itemname.* Look at this example:

IMPORT ITEMS DIRECTLY INTO YOUR PROGRAM

# import them
from moduletest import ageofqueen
from moduletest import printhello

now try using them
print ageofqueen
printhello()

What would be the point of that? It could be used to make the code a bit more user-friendly and readable. If we were to start looking at loads of module inside modules, that could also get rid of a cryptic layer or two.

Another way would be to import the contents of a module using *from modulename import* *. However, this isn't always as straightforward as we would like it to be, especially if your program contains objects that have the same name as items in your module. With a large module, this is highly likely and it can cause an awful lot of hassle. The best way is to import the module normally, without using the "from" operator, and then assign individual items to local name. Have a look at this example:

ASSIGNING ITEMS TO A LOCAL NAME

 # Assigning to a local name
timesfour = moduletest.timesfour

 # Using the local name
print timesfour(565)

In this way, you also get rid of a cryptic layer and you get all the items you need from a specific module.

That's it for this chapter, a nice easy lesson. Now you know how to organize your programs in a neat way and, hopefully, you can now see how easy it is to grow a complex program without ending up with an unreadable file that is awash with bugs.

Modules are neat ways to import code and, in the next chapter we are going to look at file Input and Output, and how to save information inside a class so that you can get at it later on.

CHAPTER 10:
FILE INPUT/OUTPUT

In the last chapter we talked about importing external code into a program so, without any further ado, let's take a look at file input and output, using normal text files and then, later on, we'll talk about how to save and restore an instance of a class.

Opening Files

If you want to open up a text file, you would use the *open()* function. You will pass parameters to the function to tell it how the file should be opened:

- R – read only
- W – writing only
- A – append (adding something to the end of a file)
- R+ for read and write

Less of the talk now, let's open up a file in read mode, using IDLE mode in Python. Open up a text file and we are then going to print what is inside it:

openfile = open('pathtofile', 'r')
openfile.read()

That was somewhat interesting wasn't it! You will notice a significant amount of \n symbols – we use these to represent newlines – where Enter is pressed to start another line. The text is not formatted but if you passed the output to print, it would be formatted in a nice neat way.

Try typing into IDLE, *print openfile.read*

What happened? It most likely failed and the reason for it is because the cursor has moved. What cursor, I hear you ask? This is a cursor that you can't really see. This invisible cursor is what tells the read function, as well as a lot of other I/O functions, where it should start from. If you want to set the place for the cursor to start from, you must use the *seek()* function. The format is *seek(offset, whence)*

Whence is actually optional and what it does is determine the start point of where to seek from. For example, if whence had a value of 0, the letters or bytes would be counted from the start. If it had a value of 1 the bytes would be counted from the current position of the cursor and, if it were 2, they would be counted from the very end of the particular file. If no value is input or whence is not used, then the value is assumed to be 0.

Offset is how we determine how from whence the cursor is going to move. For example:

- *Openfile.seek(45,0)* – this would move the cursor to a position that is 45 letters or bytes after the start of the file
- *Openfile.seek(10,1)* – this would move the cursor to a position that is 0 letters or bytes after the current position of the cursor
- *Openfile*.seek(-77,2) – this would move the cursor to a position that is 77 letters or bytes before the file end – notice that there is a – in front of the 77

Try it out for yourself now. Use the *openfile.seek()* to go to any point in your file and then use *openfile.read()*. Notice that it prints from where you seeked to but also notice that *openfile.read()* will move the cursor to end of your file and you will have to use the seek function again.

What Else Can We Do?

There are loads of different functions that can help you with files and they have loads of different uses that can make life so much easier for you. Let's look at a few more:

tell() – This one will return to the point in the file where the cursor is. It doesn't have any parameters; you just type it in. This is a very useful function as it helps you know what you are referring to and where it is, as well as being able to control the cursor. To use it, type in *fileobjectname.tell()*. Fileobjectname will be the name of the file object that you created when you first opened the file.

readline() – This function reads from the point where the cursor is right to the end of that line. Remember – this is not the edge of your screen. Where a line ends is where you have pressed Enter to start a new line. This is a useful function for reading event logs, or working through something in a progressive way. This one also has no parameters although you can, if you want, tell it the absolute maximum number of bytes or letters to read by placing the relevant number in the brackets. To use it, type *fileobjectname.readline()*.

readlines() – This is similar to readline with the exception that it will read all of the lines after the point of the cursor and will then return a list. That list contains elements that each has a line of code. To use it, type *fileobjectname.readlines()*. An example:

Line 1

Line 3
Line 4

Line 6
The list that readlines() would return would be:

Index	Value
0	'Line 1'
1	"
Index	Value
2	'Line 3'
3	'Line 4'
4	"
5	'Line 6'

write() – as you would expect, this one writes to the file. It will start from where the cursor is and then overwrite any text that is in front of it – pretty much like using the "insert" function in Microsoft Word. To use this, you must insert a string in between the brackets, telling it what to write, for example, *fileobjectname.write(this is the text to write)*

close() – closes the file so that you can't read it or write to it until you open it up again. To use it, type *fileobjectname.close()*

So, open up IDLE mode in Python, either open a test file or make a new one and then have a play around with all these functions, see what they do and how they work. They can help you to do quite a bit of text editing in an easy way.

Pickles

No, not the ones you get in a jar. In Python, a pickle is an object that has been saved to a file. It could be a variable; it could be a class instance, a list, a tuple, or a dictionary. There are other things that you can pickle but they do have limits. Once you have pickled an object, it can be unpickled, or restored, later on. In all honesty, what you are doing is saving an object, that is all.

So, how do we go about pickling an object? We use the *dump()*, which you will find residing in the pickle module. At the start of your program, you simply type *import pickle()*. Then you will open an empty file and type *pickle.dump()* to put the object into the file. Let's have a go at that:

pickletest.py
PICKLE AN OBJECT

 # import pickle module
import pickle

 # let's make something to be pickled
 # How about a list?
picklelist = ['one',2,'three','four',5,'can you count?']

 # now we create a file
 # replace the filename with the file you want to make
file = open('filename', 'w')

 # now let's pickle picklelist
pickle.dump(picklelist,file)

 # close the file, and your pickling is finished
file.close()

The code is formatted similar to *pickle.load(object_to_pickle, file_object)*:

object_to_pickle will be the object that you want to save in a file.
file_object will be the object that you write to.

When you have closed the file, open it up again in Notepad, or whatever text editor you are using, and take a look at it. You will see what looks like total gobbledygook and you will see the bits that you created.

To unpickle your object, you would type *pickle.load()*. For example:

```
### unpickletest.py
### unpickle file
# import the pickle module
import pickle

# now open a file for reading
# replace the filename with the path to the file that you created in
pickletest.py
unpicklefile = open('filename', 'r')

# now we load the list that we pickled into a new object
unpickledlist = pickle.load(unpicklefile)

# close the file, just in case you lose it
unpicklefile.close()

# Try using the list
for item in unpickledlist:
    print item
```

Isn't that neat? Of course, there is a limitation – we can only add one object into a file. The way around this would be to put loads of objects that can be pickled into a dictionary or a list and then you pickle the entire dictionary or list.

The subject of pickles goes much deeper but I just wanted to give you an overview of it so, if you come across them in your programming you will at least know what is being talked about.

CHAPTER 11:
ERROR HANDLING

So, the final thing I want to talk about is errors. I'm sure you have come across some, if not you haven't been trying hard enough! Errors or exceptions are an everyday part of programming. Take a look at this piece of code here:

```
def menu(list, question):
  for entry in list:
    print 1 + list.index(entry),
    print ") " + entry


  return input(question) - 1


# running the function
# remember what the backslash is for
answer = menu(['A','B','C','D','E','F','H','T'],\
'Which letter is your favorite one? ')


print 'You picked answer ' + (answer + 1)
```

This is probably familiar to you as it is part of the men program we wrote earlier. Looks OK, doesn't it? Now try running it and see what happens.

Human Error

The most common issues will be of your own making, sadly. Let's see what happens when we run this program:

Traceback (most recent call last):

  File "/home/steven/errortest.py", line 8, in -toplevel-

   answer = menu(< I'll snip it here >)

  File "/home/steven/errortest.py", line 6, in menu

   return raw_input(question) - 1

TypeError: unsupported operand type(s) for -: 'str' and 'int'

What on earth does all that mean? Python is trying to tell you that you can't put a number and a text string into a single text string. Let's break this error message down and see what it is all about:

File "/home.steven/errortest.py", line 8 in -toplevel – this tells us three things – first, the file the error occurred in; second, which line it is in and, third, that there is no indentation.

Answer = menu(['A', 'B', 'C', 'D', 'E', 'F', 'H', 'I'], 'Which letter is your favorite one?') - this is a duplication of the code that contains the error.

Because the error line is calling a function, the next line tells you the location in the function of the actual error:

TypeError: unsupported operand type(s) for -: 'str' and 'int' – this is telling you what the error is; a type error in this case, where you attempted to subtract variables that are not compatible.

Why are there so many error listings for one mistake? Because the error happened where two lines of code interacted. For example, the error happened on the line where you called a function and on the line inside the function itself where something went wrong.

So, we now what we did wrong, how do we go about fixing it? Because the error message has told us where the problem lies, we only have to focus on that specific piece of code: for example:

*answer = menu(['A', 'B', 'C', 'D', 'E', 'F', 'H', 'I'], *
'Which letter is your favorite one? ')

This, as you know by now, is a call to a function. The error happened on this line in the function:

return raw_input(question) - 1
raw_input will always return a string, and that is why we have a problem. Let's change it to input(), which will return a number when you input a number:

Let's fix this:

return input(question) - 1
Bug fixed!

Exceptions – Code Limitations
OK. When you do everything right and normal the program runs just fine. What if you were to do something a little bit weird? Try typing a letter in, instead of a number and see what happens:

Traceback (most recent call last):
* File "/home/steven/errortest.py", line 8, in -toplevel-*
*   answer = menu(< I'll snip it here >)*
* File "/home/steven/errortest.py", line 6, in menu*
*   return input(question) - 1*
* File "", line 0, in -toplevel-*
NameError: name 'g' is not defined

What is this telling us now? There are two error code listings – line 8 and line 6. What Python is trying to tell us is that when you called the function on line 8, something happened on line 6. This makes perfect sense when you understand how the input() function works. If you insert a letter or a word, the function immediately assumes that you are talking about a variable so, in line 6, what we are actually trying to do is subtract a number from a variable, and that doesn't work, because the variable doesn't exist.

How do we fix this one? By using two operators – *try* and *except.*

Here's an example of the *try* operator at work in our error:

```
def menu(list, question):
    for entry in the list:
        print 1 + list.index(entry),
        print ") " + entry
    try:
        return input(question) - 1
    except NameError:
        print "Enter a correct number"
```

Now try putting in a letter when you need to put in a number. We fixed that problem but we seem to have caused another one. This is always going to happen and you will sometimes feel like you're on a never-ending path, simply because your code is so messy. Let's look at the new error:

Traceback (most recent call last):
  File "/home/steven/errortest.py", line 12, in -toplevel-

print 'You picked the answer', (answer + 1)
TypeError: unsupported operand type(s) for +: 'NoneType' and 'int'

Now what has happened is that no value has been returned by the menu function, only an error message. The result we are trying to print is the returned value + 1. Because there is no returned value, we don't know what we are trying to add 1 to.

We could just have it return any number but we would be lying. What we actually have to do is rewrite it so that the program can cope with this.

 # from when we finish defining the function
answer = menu(['A','B','C','D','E','F','H','I'],
'Which letter is your favorite one? ')
try:
  print 'You picked the answer', (answer + 1)
  # you can put something after a comma in the 'print' statement,
  # and it will carry on as if you had typed in 'print' again
except:
  print '\nincorrect answer.'
  # the '\n' is for formatting reasons. Try it without and see.
Problem solved again.

Endless Errors

What we did above really isn't a recommended course of action because, apart from the very error that we now may happen, *except:* will catch every single error. This mean that we are never going to see the one error that is going to cause problems later on and we cannot possibly hope to control the errors we can deal with. We also can't deal with any more than one error type in a code block. So, what do we do? Take a look at this example of a piece of code with just such a problem:

```
print 'Subtraction program, v0.0.1 (beta)'
a = input('Enter a number to subtract from > ')
b = input('Enter the number to subtract > ')
print a - b
```

You input your numbers and everything goes well. Put in a letter and you get *NameError*. O we need to rewrite our code to deal ONLY with that NameError. We'll put it into a loop so the program will start again when the error happens. To do this, we will use *continue*, which will take the loop right back to the start, and *break*, which will leave the loop.

```
print 'Subtraction program, v0.0.2 (beta)'
loop = 1
while loop == 1:
  try:
    a = input('Enter a number to subtract from > ')
    b = input('Enter the number to subtract > ')
  except NameError:
    print "\nYou cannot subtract a letter"
  continue
  print a - b
  try:
    loop = input('Press 1 to try again > ')
  except NameError:
    loop = 0
```

We started the loop again if something was typed in wrong and, in line 12, we just assume that the program is to quit if 1 isn't entered.

There are still some problems though. If something is left blank or an odd character is input, we get a *SyntaxError*. How do we deal with that?

```
print 'Subtraction program, v0.0.3 (beta)'
loop = 1
while loop == 1:
  try:
    a = input('Enter a number to subtract from > ')
    b = input('Enter the number to subtract > ')
  except NameError:
    print "\nYou cannot subtract a letter"
      continue
  except SyntaxError:
    print "\nPlease enter a number only."
      continue
  print a - b
  try:
    loop = input('Press 1 to try again > ')
  except (NameError,SyntaxError):
    loop = 0
```

Now, you have several *except* uses, each one for a different issue. You can use one to deal with multiple issues as well, simply by putting them in parentheses and by using commas to separate them.

This program is now hard for an end user to crash – have a go and see if you can do it. If you can't, go back to the section on Human Error and have another look.

That concludes our Python programming session and I hope that you have found it useful.

CONCLUSION

Thank you again for purchasing this book!

I hope this book was able to help you to learn the basics of Python programming without too much trouble.

The next step is to move on to more complicated programming but don't make the mistake of moving on to another language at this stage. All I have given you here is the basics of Python programming, the components that make up the language. There is much more to learn on Python before you move on so use the internet, download books and get yourself on Python programming courses to learn it fully.

One more thing you must remember – practice does make perfect. It is no good learning a computer programming language like Python and then forgetting about it. Not only do things change very quickly in the word of computer programming languages, you will not remember everything you learned unless you practice regularly.

Finally, if you enjoyed this book, then I'd like to ask you for a favor, would you be kind enough to leave a review for this book on Amazon? It'd be greatly appreciated!

Click here to leave a review for this book on Amazon!

Thank you and good luck!

ATTRIBUTES

http://sthurlow.com/python/

http://www.anthonydebarros.com/2015/08/16/setting-up-python-in-windows-10/

https://docs.python.org/2/tutorial/

www.ingramcontent.com/pod-product-compliance
Lightning Source LLC
Chambersburg PA
CBHW071551080326
40690CB00056B/1788